**EUDIST PRAYERBOOK SERIES:
VOLUME 5**

On the Threshold of Life

A SELF-DIRECTED RETREAT TO CELEBRATE YOUR BIRTHDAY

by St. John Eudes

Translated from the French
by Thomas Merton
Originally published 1946
(New York: P. J. Kenedy & Sons)

Edited by Maryann Marshall and Steven S. Marshall
Layout by Deanna Heitschmidt

Cover image: a 40 ton marble statue of St. John Eudes in St. Peter's Basilica. Carved in 1932 by Silvio Silva, this is one of 39 large statues around the Basilica's nave and transepts honoring the founders of great religious orders.

ISBN: 978-0-9979114-6-6

Copyright ©2019, by
The Eudists – Congregation of Jesus and Mary

All Rights Reserved.

Published by

PO Box 3619
Vista CA 92085-3619
eudistsusa.org

No part of this publication may be reproduced in any form or by any means, including scanning, photocopying, or otherwise without prior written permission of the copyright holder: The Eudists – Congregation of Jesus and Mary.

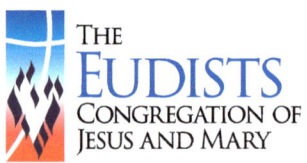

Table of Contents

Introduction 1

Exercise for the Anniversary of Your Birth 5

    Concerning the Rightful Homage You Ought
to Have Rendered to God at the Moment of
Your Birth if You Had the Use of Reason 6

    Prayer to Jesus for the Anniversary of Your Birth 7

    Prayer to the Most Blessed Virgin 11

    Prayer to Angels and Saints Whom You Were
Duty-Bound to Honor at the Time of Your Birth 12

Exercise for the Anniversary of Your Baptism 13

    Concerning the Rightful Tribute That You Should
Have Paid to God on the Day of Your Baptism 14

    Obligations to Our Lord Jesus Christ Who
Instituted and Merited Baptism for You 15

    The Eternal and Temporal Birth of Jesus, and His Death,
Burial, and Resurrection Are the Exemplar of Baptism 17

    Jesus Christ, in the Person of the Priest,
Baptizes Each Christian 20

    Solemn Profession Made by All Christians At Baptism 22

    Baptismal Tribute to The Holy Trinity 24

    Prayer to the Blessed Trinity 25

    Rosary of the Blessed Trinity 26

Conclusion 27

    Acts of Love in Honor of the Birth and
Holy Childhood of Jesus 29

Addenda 31

    A Note on the Translator 32

    About St. John Eudes 34

    About the Eudist Family 38

Introduction

No one has the use of reason at his or her birth, and few can exercise reason at their Baptism, since many of us were baptized as infants. St. John Eudes invites — even insists — that each year on the anniversaries of these events to renew our devotion to Jesus. In *The Life and the Kingdom of Jesus*, Father Eudes offers this passage on Christian Devotion. He goes on after this passage to speak of the forming of Jesus in the Christian soul.

Later in the same work the saint offers advice about commemorating these important anniversaries.

From St. John Eudes' own pen:

True Christian Devotion

After what has been said so far about Christian virtues, it is easy to see what true Christian devotion is and in what it consists. Since all the Christian virtues are nothing else but the virtues which our Lord Jesus Christ practiced on earth, which must be continued by us while we are in this world, it necessarily follows that true Christian devotion is simply Jesus Christ's holy and divine devotion, that we are bound to perpetuate and fulfil in ourselves.

Now, for our Lord Jesus Christ, devotion was a matter of accomplishing, with the greatest perfection, everything that His Father willed, and of taking all His pleasure in this alone. His devotion consisted in serving His heavenly Father, and in serving even men for the love of His Father, since He willed to take the form and lowly condition of a servant in order to pay more honor and homage to the supreme greatness of His Father by His own abasement. His devotion consisted in loving and glorifying His Father and in causing His Father to be loved and glorified in the world; of doing all that He did purely for the glory and love of His Father with most holy, most pure and most divine dispositions — namely, with the most profound humility, the most burning charity for men, the most perfect detachment from self and from all created things, the closest union with His heavenly Father, the most rigorous submission to His Father's will, and with all joy and satisfaction. Finally, His devotion consisted in being altogether immolated and sacrificed purely for the glory of His Father, since He willed to take upon Himself the role of victim, and in this capacity to undergo every sort of contempt, humiliation, privation, interior and exterior mortification and, finally, a cruel and shameful death. for the everlasting glory of His divine Father.

These were three solemn professions, three vows, as it were, pronounced by Jesus from the moment of the incarnation. These He carried out most perfectly in His life and in His death.

1. At the moment of His incarnation, He vowed obedience to His Father, that is, He made profession never to do His own will, but to obey most perfectly everything willed by His Father, and to find in so doing all His bliss and joy.

2. He professed servitude to His Father. This is the character given to Him by His Father, speaking through a prophet:

"You are my servant, O Israel, for in you will I glory" (Isa. 49:3).

This is the character which He Himself adopts:

"...the form of a servant" (Phil. 2:7),

lowering Himself to the state and condition of a humble and servile life with respect to His creatures, even to the cruel shame and servile death of the cross, for love of us and for His Father's glory.

3. He professed to become a host and victim entirely consecrated and immolated to His Father's glory from the first moment of His life to the very last.

Such was the devotion of Jesus. Since Christian devotion is simply Jesus Christ's devotion, our own devotion must, therefore, consist of similar vows of submission. In order to make it so, we should enter into the closest and most intimate contact and union with Jesus, and adhere to Him most closely, concentrating upon Him all our attention, throughout our whole life, in all our functions and acts.

This is the solemn vow, the first and most important public profession, which is made at Baptism in the presence of the entire Church. At that time, to use the terms of St. Augustine, St. Thomas' Summa, and the Catechism of the Council of Trent, we made a solemn vow and profession to renounce satan with all his works and to be united with Jesus Christ as members are one with their head, to deliver and consecrate ourselves entirely to Him and to dwell in Him. A Christian who professes to adhere to Christ and dwell in Him, professes to adhere to His devotion, His dispositions, His intentions, His laws and rules of conduct, His spirit and His behavior, His life, His qualities, and His virtues, and all that He did and suffered.

Thus, when we vow to adhere to Jesus Christ and dwell in Him, this is

> "the greatest of all our vows," says St. Augustine.

We make three great professions, which are very sacred and sublime, deserving frequent consideration.

1. We profess, with Jesus Christ, never to do our own will but to submit to everything willed by God, to obey persons of all kinds, in whatever is not contrary to God, and to seek all our satisfaction and heavenly bliss in acting so.

2. We profess servitude to God and His Son Jesus Christ, and to all the members of Jesus Christ, according to the words of St. Paul:

> "...ourselves your servants through Jesus" (II Cor. 4:5).

In consequence of this avowal, no Christian can call anything his own, any more than a slave can. Nor has a Christian the right to make any use of the faculties of his soul, or of his life, or his daily time, or his temporal goods, except for Jesus Christ and the members of Jesus Christ — that is, all who believe in Him.

3. We profess to become victims continually sacrificed to God's glory —

> "...spiritual sacrifices..." (1 Pet. 2:5), as St. Peter, the prince of the Apostles, expresses it.

Says St. Paul:

> "I beseech you therefore, brethren, by the mercy of God, that you present your bodies as a living sacrifice, holy, pleasing to

God" (Rom. 12:1).

What is here said of our bodies must also be said of our souls. So we are obliged to glorify and love God, in proportion to all the powers of our body and soul, to do everything possible that He may be glorified and loved, and in all our acts and in all things to seek nothing but His glory alone, His love alone, and to live in such a way that each Christian life may be a ceaseless sacrifice of praise and love. We should be ready to be completely immolated and consumed for His glory.

In a word:

"Christianity is the profession of the life of Christ," says St. Gregory of Nyssa.

St. Bernard assures us that our Lord does not admit to the ranks of those professed in His religion. Anyone who does not live His life:

"...does not count among those who profess his name. He sees them as deserters."

That is why we profess Jesus Christ at holy Baptism. We profess the life of Christ, Christ's devotion, His dispositions and intentions, His virtues and His perfect detachment from all things. We profess to believe firmly everything that He teaches, either by His own words and example or through His Church, and to choose death before swerving, however little, from this belief. We profess to join Him in a fight to the finish with sin; to live as He lived, in a spirit of uninterrupted prayer; to carry His cross with Him, as well as to bear His mortification in our bodies and souls; to continue the practice of His humility, His trust in God, His submissiveness and obedience, His charity and zeal for the glory of His Father and the salvation of souls. We profess to live, on earth and in heaven, only in order to belong to Jesus and to love and honor Him in all the states and mysteries of His life, in all that He is, in Himself and in the universe. Finally, we profess to be ever ready to undergo every form of torture and to die a thousand deaths, if it were possible, purely for His love and for His glory.

Such are the vow and profession made by all Christians at their Baptism. This is what constitutes true Christian devotion. Any other devotion, if it be possible for any other to exist, is mere deception and perdition.

Exercise for the Anniversary of Your Birth

Concerning the Rightful Homage You Ought to Have Rendered to God at the Moment of Your Birth if You Had the Use of Reason

I can never tell you enough, nor should you grow tired of hearing and considering (so important is it) that Jesus Christ, Who is your head and Whose members you are, passed through all the stages of human life through which you are passing. He did almost all the things that you do, and performed not only His outward acts but also all His interior actions for Himself and for you. Therefore, Christian sanctity and perfection consist in ceaselessly uniting yourself to Him as His members, and in continuing to do what He did, as He did it, to the best of your ability, uniting yourself with His dispositions and intentions. It likewise consists in consenting and adhering to what He did for you in the presence of His Father and in ratifying it. So, too, it consists in performing all your inward actions not only for yourself, but also for the whole world, in imitation of the Son of God, and especially for those with whom you have some special connection with respect to God. This Christian devotion inspires similar acts of union and imitation proportionately towards the blessed Virgin, never separating the Mother from the Son. You will gain a clearer idea of this from reflecting upon the devotion you should have paid Him from the very first moment of your life and at the instant of your birth on earth if you had enjoyed the use of reason.

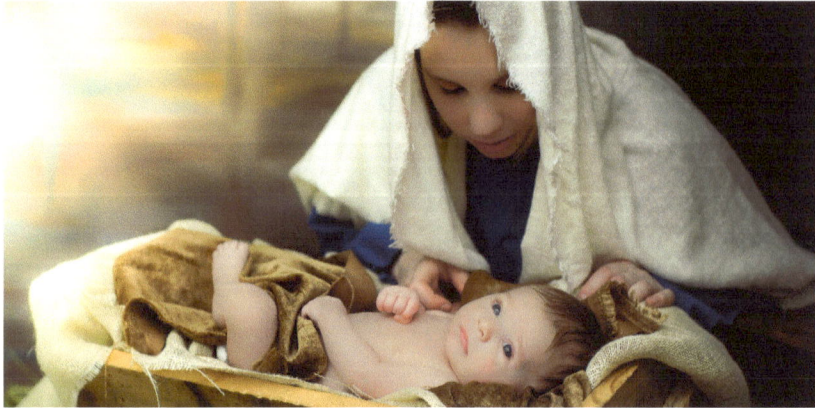

Prayer to Jesus for the Anniversary of Your Birth

O Jesus, I adore You in Your eternal birth and Your divine dwelling for all eternity in the bosom of Your Father. I also adore You in Your temporal conception, and in Your presence in the sacred womb of Your most pure Mother, for the space of nine months, and in Your birth into this world at the end of that time. I adore and revere the great and admirable occurrence of all these mysteries. I adore and honor the holy dispositions of Your divine person and Your holy soul in these mysteries. with my whole heart I adore, love and bless all the acts of adoration, love, and oblation You rendered to the eternal Father, and all the other divine acts and practices offered Him in these mysteries.

Again I adore and glorify You, O good Jesus, as performing all these things for Yourself, for me, and for everyone in the world. On this anniversary of my birth I give myself to You, O my dear Jesus, that I may now repeat the acts You perfected while dwelling from all eternity in the bosom of the Father, and for nine months in the bosom of Your Mother. I unite myself to You to perform this duty as You performed it, in union with the love, humility, purity, and other holy dispositions of Your adorable soul.

Since You performed this act for Yourself and for me and for all men in the world, I also desire to exercise this present devotion, not only for myself, but for all the men in the world.

I now desire, O my Savior, to render unto You as far as I can, with the help of Your grace, all the rightful homage I should have paid You if I had been gifted with the use of reason from the first moment of my life. So, too, I desire to pay You all the due need of adoration, praise, and love which should have been given to You at that same time by all my friends, and by all people who ever were, are, or shall be in the world; and even that which should have been rendered to You by the evil angels at the moment of their creation.

I give myself again to You, my Lord Jesus. Enter into me, and unite me to Yourself in order that in and by You I may fulfil these desires for Your pure glory and satisfaction.

In union, therefore, with the devotion, love, humility, purity, and sanctity, and all the other sublime dispositions with which You honored, blessed, loved and glorified the eternal Father in Your eternal and temporal birth, and in Your dwelling from all eternity in the bosom of Your Father, and during nine months in the bosom of Your Mother: I acclaim You: I adore, love, bless, and glorify You together with the Father and the Holy Spirit as my God, my Creator and sovereign Lord. I adore, love, and glorify You also on behalf of all creatures – angels, men, animals, plants, and inanimate things. I wish I could possess in myself the totality of their being, all their strength, and all their actual or potential capacity to glorify and love You, that I might now use it all in paying You this homage for myself and for them, especially those for whom, before You, I have both the obligation and desire to pray with special zeal.

I give You infinite thanks, O my God, on behalf of myself, all creatures, and especially my particular friends, for the gift of life, and the capacity to know and love You. I thank You for having preserved our existence and allowed us to be born alive to receive holy Baptism. If we had died before being delivered from original sin by the grace of holy Baptism, which has been the misfortune of many souls, we should never have seen Your divine face, and we should have been deprived forever of Your holy love. May all the angels and saints bless You forever for this most special favor You have accorded us.

Omnipotent Creator, You gave me being and life solely that I might employ them in Your love and service. Therefore, I offer my life to You. I consecrate and sacrifice it altogether to You, together with the being and life of all the angels, all men and all creatures, in testimony that I desire no longer to live save to serve You with all the perfection You ask of me.

O my God, what a source of humiliation and pain it is for me to think that, during the first months of my life, I was Your enemy and under the power of satan, and in a continual state of sin that infinitely displeased and dishonored You! For this I most humbly beg Your forgiveness, O my Lord, and in satisfaction for the dishonor I gave You while I remained in the state of original sin, I offer You, O Father of Jesus, all the glory given You by Your immaculate Mother during the time she dwelt in the blessed womb of St. Anne, her mother.

O my Jesus, in honor of and in union with the love with which You accepted and bore all the crosses and sufferings that were permitted by the heavenly Father to attend Your temporal birth, I offer You all the trials and afflictions I have suffered since my birth, and those remaining for me to suffer until the end of my life, accepting and loving them for love of You, and begging You to consecrate them to the homage of Your own sufferings.

O most kind Jesus, I offer You all the circumstances of my birth, and I implore You by Your very great mercy to wipe out all that displeases You in the first part of my life. Deign to make up for my faults, giving to Your Father and to Yourself all the honor I ought to have given You at that time, if I had been capable of honoring You; and may You grant that the earliest phase of my life may render an undying homage and glory to the divine state of Your dwelling in the bosom of Your Father and in the womb of Your Mother, and to Your eternal and temporal birth.

Such, O my Lord, is the rightful homage I ought to have rendered to You, had I been able, at the moment of my birth, and indeed from the first moment of my life, that I now endeavor to render to You, although very tardily and imperfectly. What gives me infinite consolation, O my dear Jesus, is that I know You atoned for my deficiencies by Your temporal birth. Then You rendered all this just homage to God the Father, performing in a most holy and divine manner all these acts and devotions for Yourself and for me. You referred and consecrated to His glory all Your being and Your entire life, present and to come, and together with it all my being and every state of my life, and of all creatures that ever were, are, or shall be, all the past, present, and future state of created things being just as vividly present to You then as now. You looked upon every life as Your own, as something given to You by the Father, according to Your blessed words:

All things are delivered to Me by My Father (Matt. 11:27).

You were consequently obliged by Your profound love for Him and Your zeal for His honor, to refer and give and sacrifice everything to Him. This You did most excellently.

You also offered to Your Father the holy and divine state of Your dwelling in the sacred womb of the Virgin, all filled with glory and love for Him, in satisfaction for the dishonor that was to be rendered to Him by myself in the state of original sin. At the same moment when You accepted and offered to Your Father all the crosses and sufferings of Your whole life, You offered Him also all the past, present, and future trials and afflictions of all Your members: for it is the function of the head to act for Himself and on behalf of all His members, because the head and the members are but one, and also because all that pertains to the members belongs to the head, and conversely all the attributes of the head belong to the members.

So, O divine Head, You have turned my whole being and the whole condition of my life to meritorious purpose. In Your temporal birth, You rendered for me to Your Father all the rightful homage I should have rendered Him at my own birth, and You then practiced all the acts and exercises of devotion that I should have practiced. Be blessed for ever! How willingly I consent and adhere to all that You did at that time for me! Indeed I ratify it with my whole will, and would gladly sign that ratification with the last drop of my blood. I also endorse all You did for me in all the other phases or actions of Your life, to compensate for the faults You knew I was going to commit.

In imitation of You, O my Jesus, in honor of and in union with the same love which led You thus to accomplish all things for Yourself and for all Your brothers, members, and children, and for all creatures, I henceforth desire in all my functions and activities to render to You all the honor and glory I can, for myself and for all Christians, who are my brothers and members of the same head and body. I desire to honor You on behalf of all men and all other creatures that are unworthy or incapable of loving You, as if all of them put together had entrusted me with their duties and obligations towards You and had charged me to love and honor You on their behalf.

A Self-Directed Retreat to Celebrate your Birthday

Prayer to the Most Blessed Virgin

O Mother of Jesus, I honor you, as far as I am able, in the moment of your holy conception, and in the instant of your birth into the world. I honor all the love, all the adoration, praise, oblations, and blessings you offered to God at that time. In union with your love, purity, and humility as you adored, loved, and glorified Him, and referred your being and your life to Him, I adore, bless, and love my God, with you, my Mother, with my whole heart. I consecrate and sacrifice to Him forever my life, my being, and my whole self.

So also, acclaiming you, O Blessed Virgin, as Mother of God and consequently as my sovereign Lady, I refer to you, after God, the whole state of my being and my life. I implore you most humbly to offer to God, for me, all the love, the glory, and rightful homage you rendered to Him at your birth, by way of satisfaction for my faults, and to cause, by your prayers and merits, all the phases, actions, and sufferings of my life to pay undying homage to all the phases, actions, and sufferings of your Son's life and Your own.

Prayer to Angels and Saints Whom You Were Duty-Bound to Honor at the Time of Your Birth

Having acquitted yourself in the above manner of your rightful tribute of homage to our Lord and His blessed Mother, you should offer your salutations and pay your respects to the holy guardian angel assigned to you by God when you were born; to the guardian angels of your father and mother, of the house, the place, and the diocese where you were born; to the order of angels with whom God plans to associate you in heaven; also to the saints of the day, the place, and the district where you were born. You should thank them for their helpful favors, offer yourself to their honor all your life long according to God's holy will. You should ask them to offer you to our Lord, to use you as an instrument for His glory, and to render to Him all the due tribute of homage you should have paid Him at your birth. Invoke these devoted guardians frequently to obtain by their prayers fresh grace and new strength for you to begin a new life, which may be totally consecrated to their glory and the glory of the God of angels and saints.

Exercise for the Anniversary of Your Baptism

Concerning the Rightful Tribute That You Should Have Paid to God on the Day of Your Baptism

Holy Baptism is the beginning of your true life, that is, your life in Jesus Christ, and it is the origin of all happiness. Therefore, it is certain that you would have been obliged to render a very special tribute to your heavenly Father on the occasion of your Baptism. However you were incapable of fulfilling your obligation then because you did not have the use of reason. It is logical that you should each year set apart a little interval near the anniversary of your Baptism, or else some other time, to devote yourself to prayer and thanksgiving for this priceless sacrament.

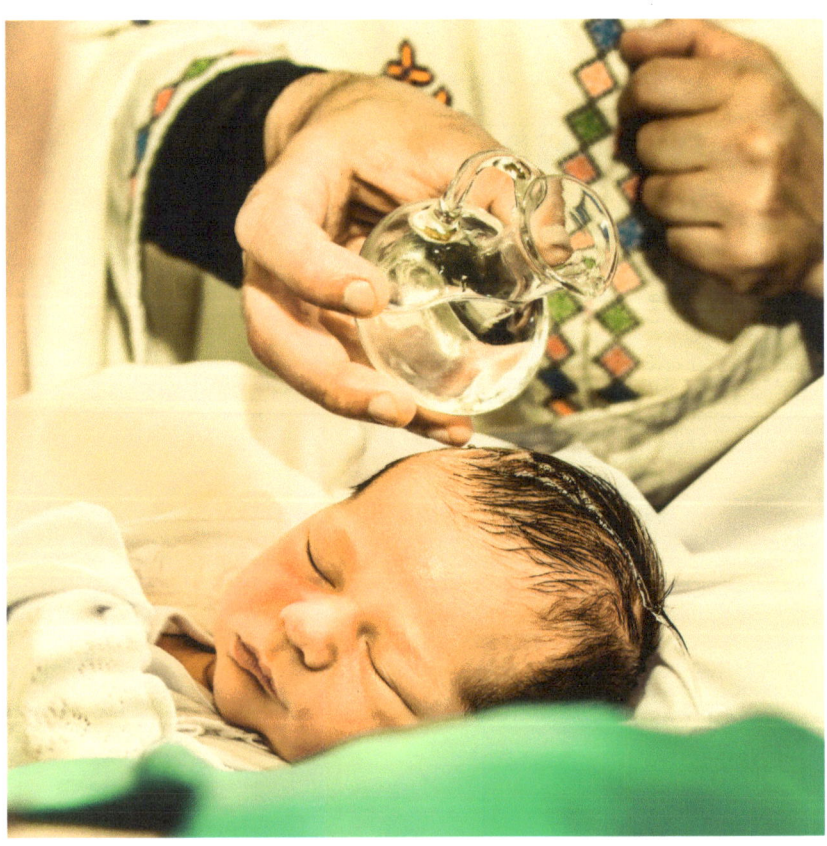

A Self-Directed Retreat to Celebrate your Birthday

Obligations to Our Lord Jesus Christ Who Instituted and Merited Baptism for You

The author of the holy sacrament of Baptism is Jesus Christ our Lord. He is the source of all its graces, acquired and merited by His incarnation, by His baptism in the River Jordan, by His passion and death. He applied these infinite merits to you by virtue of His resurrection, out of His exceeding great love.

All those invaluable blessings require you to pay Him the tribute of respect expressed in the following prayer.

Prayer

O Jesus, I adore You as divine author of the holy sacrament of Baptism, which You instituted for my salvation. You also acquired and merited the grace contained in that sacrament, by Your incarnation, Your Baptism in the River Jordan, and by Your holy death. I adore the exceeding great love with which You merited and instituted this same sacrament. I adore all the designs which You cherished in its institution, for the whole Church and for myself in particular.

I thank You countless times for all the glory You have given to Yourself and for all the graces You have transmitted to Your Church, and to me in particular, by this sacrament. I offer You all that glory and all the graces You have produced in Your holy Church by this means. I beg You to forgive me for neglecting to take advantage of the grace You gave me in holy Baptism, and for having made it valueless by my cowardice and infidelities in Your service, and for having even destroyed it entirely in my soul, by my sins. I give myself to You, O good Jesus; renew in me the treasure of baptismal grace, and accomplish in me, by Your very great mercy, all the plans of Your providence on my behalf in the divine sacrament of Baptism.

O Jesus, I adore You in the mystery of Your incarnation, passion, and death as meriting the grace of the sacrament of Baptism; but especially do I adore You in the mystery of Your holy Baptism in the River Jordan. I adore all the dispositions of Your divine soul in this mystery, and all the designs You then deigned to have in my regard. How different was Your Baptism, Lord, from ours! In Your Baptism You took upon Yourself our sins, to make satisfaction and do penance for them before the Father of heaven, in the desert and on the cross, while in our Baptism You lifted from us the burden of our sins, washing and effacing them in Your precious blood. Baptize me with the baptism of the Holy Spirit and of fire, even as Your blessed precursor, St. John the Baptist, assures us You do baptize, that is, consume all my sins in the fire of Your holy love, and by the power of Your divine Spirit.

The Eternal and Temporal Birth of Jesus, and His Death, Burial, and Resurrection Are the Exemplar of Baptism

All things outside of God have their idea, their exemplar, and their prototype in God; so also sacramental Baptism has for prototype and exemplar four great mysteries, namely:

1. The mystery of His eternal birth, because His Father, by eternal generation, imparted to Him being, life, and all the divine perfections, by reason of which He is the Son of God and the perfect image of His Father. Likewise, by Baptism He imparted to you the celestial and divine life He received from His Father; He implanted in you a living image of Himself, and He made you children of His own heavenly Father.

2. The mystery of His temporal birth, because at the moment of His incarnation and birth in the Virgin, He united our nature with Himself and Himself with our nature, and filled it with Himself and clad Himself in it as in a garment; similarly in the holy sacrament of Baptism He united Himself with you and incorporated you with Him; He formed Himself and, as it were, took flesh in you. He clothed and filled you with Himself, according to these words of St. Paul:

"As many of you as have been baptized in Christ have put on Christ" (Gal. 3:27).

3. The mystery of His death and burial, for St. Paul also tells us that

"All we who are baptized in Christ Jesus, are baptized in His death." (Rom. 6:3)

and that

"We are buried together with Him by baptism into death." (Rom. 6:4).

This means precisely the same as the thought expressed by the same apostle in other words:

"You are dead: and your life is hid with Christ in God." (Col. 3:3)

That is, you have entered by Baptism into a state which obliges you to die to yourself and to the world, and to live no longer except with Jesus Christ, by a totally holy and divine life, hidden and absorbed in God, resembling the life of Jesus Christ.

4. The mystery of the resurrection, because by His resurrection the Son of God entered into a new life, totally heavenly and spiritual, entirely separated from the earth. So St. Paul instructs the faithful:

"We are buried together with Him by Baptism into death; that as Christ is risen from the dead by the glory of the Father, so we also may walk in newness of life." (Rom. 6:4)

For these reasons, then, we owe our Savior a great tribute of homage and should lift up our minds and hearts to Him.

Prayer to Jesus

O Jesus, Son of God and at the same time Son of man, I adore You in Your temporal and eternal birth. I give You infinite thanks for all the glory You thus rendered to Your Father. I adore the thoughts and designs You then deigned to have for me, thinking of me from the very first, O good Jesus: You loved me and planned to make in me a living image of Yourself, of Your birth, and Your life. Just as Your Father communicates to You His divine and immortal life, and just as You are consequently His Son and His most perfect image, so also you planned to transmit to me by Baptism Your holy and celestial life, and to make me a living image of Yourself, and to transform me by grace into what You are by nature, that is, a child of God, and by participation and resemblance, God and another Jesus Christ. Who could ever thank You for such great favors! How culpable I am for having, by my sins, so often impeded the perfect fulfilment of Your divine plan! Forgive me, my Savior, with all my heart I beg You to forgive me, and I give myself to You so that You may make amends for my faults and renew in me that image of Yourself, of Your birth, and of Your life.

Separate me from myself and from all that is not You, in order to unite and incorporate me with You. Empty me of myself and of all things, destroy me utterly, in order to fill me with Yourself and to form and establish Yourself in me. Cause me henceforth to be a perfect image of Yourself, just as You are a most perfect image of Your Father. Grant that I may share in Your filial love for Him, since He is my Father as He is Yours; enable me to live by Your life, that is, a holy and perfect life, truly worthy of God, since You have made me God by participation; and, finally, invest me so fully with Your qualities, perfections, virtues, and dispositions, and so transform me into You that men may see only Jesus in me, only His life, His humility, His meekness, His charity, His love, His Spirit, and His other virtues and qualities, since You will me to be Your other self on earth.

O Jesus, I adore You in the mystery of Your holy death, Your burial and resurrection. I give You thanks for the glory You gave Your Father in these mysteries, and for the thoughts and plans You had in them for me. For You always thought of me in all these mysteries, and at every moment of Your life, and You always have a special plan for me. Your special providence was to imprint on my soul, by holy Baptism, an image of Your death, burial, and resurrection, causing me to die to myself and to the world, hiding me in Yourself, and with You in the bosom of the eternal Father, and raising me up again and causing me to live like You a new life, altogether celestial and divine. For this, be You blessed forever. Alas, by my sins I have destroyed in myself the great effects produced by Your goodness, and for this I beg You, with all humility and contrition, to forgive me. I give myself to You, O good Jesus, I surrender myself to the spirit and the power of the mystery of Your death, burial, and resurrection, that You may cause me to die again to all things; that You may hide me in Yourself and with Yourself in the bosom of Your Father; that You may dissolve my mind in Your mind, my heart in Your heart, my soul in Your soul, my life in Your life; and that You may establish in me the new life into which You entered by Your resurrection, so that I may no longer live, save in You, for You, and by You.

Jesus Christ, in the Person of the Priest, Baptizes Each Christian

All the holy Fathers teach us that our Lord Jesus Christ, Himself, by the power of His Holy Spirit, confers all the sacraments in the person of the priest, who represents Him and acts in His name and by His authority. It is He who consecrates in holy Mass and gives us absolution in the sacrament of Penance; also He baptizes us with various symbolic ceremonies, inspired by His Spirit in Holy Mother Church and filled with mysteries that signify great graces that are conferred upon us in holy Baptism. We should, therefore, pay Him homage in this connection.

Prayer to Jesus Christ Who Baptized You

O my most beloved Jesus, I adore and recognize You as the One who baptized me, in the person of the priest, whom You used as a living instrument to confer this grace upon me. Alas, Lord, I knew You not at that time: I did not think of You, I did not love You, nor did I appreciate the very great favor conferred upon me. Yet this did not deter You from loving me and receiving me among the number of Your children, and even of Your members, by the sanctifying grace of Baptism. O my adorable Savior, I desire with all my heart to bring back that holy time, that happy moment in which You baptized me, in order that I may adore, bless, love and glorify You infinitely, imploring Your eternal Father, Your Holy Spirit, Your blessed Mother, all the angels and saints and all creatures to love, bless and thank You for me forever.

O Jesus, I adore You as the One who, by Your Holy Spirit, instituted and inspired in Your Church all the ceremonies which accompany the solemn administration of sacramental Baptism. I adore all Your admirable designs in their institution. I give myself to You that You may effect them in my person, and that by Your great mercy You may produce in me the great and holy effects signified by these symbolic ceremonies.

O Jesus, cast out the evil spirit from me forever and fill me with Your divine Spirit. Give me a lively and perfect faith. Fortify my bodily senses and my spiritual faculties against every kind of temptation by the virtue of Your holy cross, and consecrate them to Your glory. Fill my soul with Your divine wisdom, that is, with Yourself. Excite in me the most avid hunger, thirst, and desire for You, the principal and only food of my soul, so that I may no longer find any savor or relish in anything save You alone. Keep me safe in Your Church, as in the bosom of a mother, apart from whom there is no life or salvation, and give me the grace to honor her in all her observances, as in customs taught and inspired by You. Give me the grace to obey all her laws and commandments, as those of a mother most worthy of honor who commands me nothing save in Your name. In all things and everywhere teach me to follow the maxims and guidance of her Spirit, which is entirely Your own.

O good Jesus, open my ears to Your word and Your voice, as You opened the ears of a man possessed by the deaf and dumb spirit, by the application of Your sacred spittle, and close them altogether to the voice of the world and of Satan. Anoint me with the oil of Your grace so that I may spread abroad, as it were, the divine odor of You in every place. Give me a firm and lasting peace with You and with every kind of creature. Clothe me in the white robe of Your holy innocence and divine purity, both bodily and spiritual.

Dispel the shadows of my darkness, filling me with Your heavenly radiance. Set me on fire with Your sacred love and cause me to be a shining and a burning light, to illumine and enkindle all my associates with the light of Your knowledge and the fire of Your love. Finally, if I was a source of joy to all the citizens of heaven, to the blessed Virgin, the eternal Father, Yourself, and the Holy Spirit, when by Baptism I was delivered from the power of satan and admitted into the divine company of angels and saints, and even of the three divine and eternal Persons, and if in token of this joy the church bells were rung after I was baptized, cause me now to live henceforth in such a way as to continue to be a source of joy and satisfaction to the court of heaven, the Queen of Angels and the most blessed Trinity. Grant also that I may find all my satisfaction and joy in serving and loving You.

Solemn Profession Made by All Christians At Baptism

I have in another place explained the nature of the solemn and public profession made by all Christians at Baptism. For that reason I need not repeat what has already been said, but it would be worth your while to refer to it again in Part One of *The Life and the Kingdom of Jesus*. I shall confine myself now to recommending a prayer to Jesus Christ in renewal of the profession made to Him at Baptism, and as a repetition in your own person of the Christian vows pronounced on your behalf then by your sponsors.

Renewal Of Baptismal Vows

O Jesus, my Lord and my God, I adore You as the mystical head Whom I must follow and imitate in all things, according to my solemn and public profession made at Baptism. I promised, through my sponsors, before heaven and earth, to renounce satan utterly with all his works and his pomps, that is, sin and the world, and to adhere to You as my head, and to give and consecrate myself altogether to You, to dwell in You forever. Great indeed are this promise and profession, which oblige me as a Christian, to practice great perfection and sanctity. To profess to dwell in You and to adhere to You as my head is to profess to be one with You, as the members are one with their head, it is to promise to have but one life, one mind, one heart, one soul, one will, one thought, one devotion, and [one] disposition with You. It means to profess not merely poverty, chastity, and obedience, but to profess Your very Self, that is, Your life, spirit, humility, charity, purity, poverty, obedience, and all other virtues. In a word, it is to make the very profession You made before the eternal Father at the moment of the incarnation, a profession perfectly fulfilled throughout Your life. It means to make profession never to follow one's own will, but to seek all happiness in doing everything willed by God, to remain in a state of perpetual subjection to God, and submissive to men for the love of God. It means existing always as a host and victim continually sacrificed to the pure glory of God. Such is the vow I made at Baptism, O Jesus my Lord. How holy and divine is that profession! How far is my life from this sanctity and perfection! How often have I failed in every respect to live up to so sacred a promise! Forgive me, most merciful Lord, forgive me. O divine Redeemer, I implore You to repair all my failings, and in satisfaction for them to offer to Your Father the inestimable honor You accorded Him all Your life long, by carrying out perfectly the profession made to Him at the incarnation.

O my Jesus, in honor of and in union with the very great love and holy dispositions of Your profession, I now desire to enact in my own person what I promised through others at my Baptism, that is, I will to renew the profession then made by my godparents. Therefore, in the virtue and might of Your spirit and Your love, I forever renounce satan, sin, the world, and myself. I give myself to You, O Jesus, to adhere to You, to remain in You, to be but one with You in heart, mind, spirit and life. I offer myself to You, never to do my own will, but to seek all my happiness in doing everything commanded by Your holy will. I sacrifice myself to You as a host and victim to be immolated to Your pure glory in any way that may be pleasing to You. O most compassionate Jesus, I implore You by Your great mercy, grant me the grace to carry out this holy profession perfectly. Fulfill it Yourself in me and for me, or rather for Yourself and for Your own good pleasure, in all the perfection You desire; for I offer myself to You to do and suffer whatever pleases You for this intention.

Baptismal Tribute to The Holy Trinity

As has been said, it is our Lord Jesus Christ who baptizes the faithful, but each soul is baptized in the name and by the power of the most holy Trinity. The three divine Persons are present at holy Baptism in a particular manner.

The Father is present generating His Son in the soul and imparting to it a new being and new life in His Son.

The Son is present, being born and receiving life in the soul, transmitting His divine Sonship, by which the neophyte becomes a child of God, just as He is Son of God.

The Holy Spirit is present, forming Jesus in each soul even as He was formed in the bosom of the Virgin.

The Father, Son and Holy Spirit are present, separating the new-born Christian from all things, taking possession of him and consecrating him specially to Themselves, imprinting Their divine character and image on his soul and establishing in his being (as in Their living temple, Their sacred tabernacle, or Their holy throne [in] heaven) the dwelling place of the blessed Trinity, Their glory, kingdom and life. Consequently, if only sin did not stand in the way, the three eternal Persons would dwell always in each Christian heart in a particular and ineffable manner; They would most wonderfully glorify one another by living in the soul a most holy and divine life. So, too, it follows that we belong to God as creatures entirely consecrated to Him and we must consequently pursue no other purpose in life save His glory and service. In this connection it would be well to pay the following tribute of praise to the holy Trinity.

Prayer to the Blessed Trinity

O holy and adorable Trinity, I adore Your divine essence and Your three eternal Persons; I adore You for having been present at my Baptism; I adore all the designs of Your providence for me. I beg You to forgive me for impeding their fulfillment, and in satisfaction I offer You the life, actions, and sufferings of my Lord Jesus Christ and of His most holy Mother. I give myself to You, O divine Trinity, for the accomplishment of those same designs.

O eternal Father, O Only Son of God, O Holy Spirit of the Father and the Son, enter into me; enter into my heart and my soul; separate me from all that is not Yourself, draw me to Yourself, live and reign in me, destroy in me all that displeases You, and cause my being and my life to be completely consecrated to Your pure glory.

Rosary of the Blessed Trinity

During the time devoted to the commemoration of the day of your Baptism in the name of the most holy Trinity, it would be a good thing to pay particular honor to that great mystery by saying the Rosary of the most holy Trinity, which is made up of three decades and three beads in honor of the three divine Persons.

First, say three times the words:

Come, holy Trinity,

to invoke in your memory, understanding and will the Father, Son, and Holy Spirit, and to give yourself to Them that They may glorify Themselves in you as They will.

On each small bead, say:

Glory be to the Father, and to the Son, and to the Holy Spirit, as it was in the beginning, is now and will be forever. Amen.

offering to the Father, Son, and Holy Spirit all the glory that has been rendered to Them from all eternity by Their own divinity and all that shall be rendered to Them for all eternity in heaven and on earth by way of satisfaction for the faults you have committed against Their honor.

On the large beads, say, with the same intention, the words:

Praise be to You, glory to You, love to You, O blessed Trinity.

CONCLUSION

To conclude the exercise on holy Baptism, thank our Lord for the graces He has imparted during this exercise, asking Him to forgive you for the faults you have committed in it. Offer yourself to the blessed Virgin, to your guardian angel, to the holy angels who were present at your Baptism, to the saint whose name you were given, and to all the other angels and saints.

Ask them to offer you to Jesus, to thank Him for you, to pay Him on your behalf all the rightful tribute of homage you would have rendered Him at the time of your Baptism if you had had the use of reason. Invoke their generous intercession to obtain from Him the grace to carry out perfectly all the holy desires and resolutions our Lord has inspired in your heart during this exercise.

A Self-Directed Retreat to Celebrate your Birthday

Acts of Love in Honor of the Birth and Holy Childhood of Jesus

[Editor's note: These prayers, penned by St. John Eudes, were introduced in *The Life and the Kingdom of Jesus.* They are included here to enhance your observance of this exercise.]

O Jesus, You are infinite love in all the moments, states, and mysteries of Your life, but, above all, You are pure love and sweetness, at the moment of Your birth and during Your most holy childhood.

Let me love You at this precious moment, in this hidden state. May heaven and earth join with me and may the whole world be transformed into love for its Creator and God, Who is completely transformed into gentleness and love for the world.

O most amiable Child, You are born by love, in love and for love. At the moment of Your birth You love Your eternal Father more than all angels and men together could do in all eternity. So, too, the heavenly Father loves You more at this moment than He ever did or will love all men and angels together.

O Jesus, I offer You all the love concentrated on You at birth by Your eternal Father, by Your Holy Spirit, Your blessed Mother, St. Joseph, St. Gabriel and all the angels and saints who participated so intimately in this most lovable mystery.

O love of Jesus, that triumphs over Him in all His mysteries, but particularly in His sublime childhood and the consummation of His cross, O Love that in these two mysteries transforms His omnipotence into helplessness, His plenitude into poverty, His sovereignty into dependence, His eternal wisdom into infancy, His joy and bliss into sufferings, and His life into death, conquer my selflove, my own will and my passions, and put me in a state of powerlessness, indigence, dependence, holy and divine childhood, and death to the world and to myself, which state may adore and glorify the powerlessness, the dependence, childhood, and death to which You reduced my Jesus in the mysteries of His nativity and of His cross.

30

ADDENDA

A Note on the Translator

In late 1941, the young **Thomas Merton** left his existence in the world to seek the freedom of cloistered life.

At the Trappist Abbey of Our Lady of Gethsemani novices were immersed in work and silence for two years before beginning serious study. Because of his mastery of language, one assignment given to the young frater (as novices were then called) was to translate certain spiritual classics from French. During Lent of 1943, he was given *The Life and Kingdom of Jesus* by St. John Eudes with an aggressive deadline for completion. His early autobiography describes the harrowing work:

> "After the Conventual Mass, I would get out book and pencil and papers and go to work at one of the long tables in the novitiate scriptorium, filling the yellow sheets as fast as I could, while another novice took them and typed them as soon as they were finished."[1]

Despite this pressure from the publisher, the project was completed on time. Merton's superior called the finished product "the best translation of any of the works of St. John Eudes that he had seen."[2] Archbishop Fulton Sheen agreed in his introduction to this edition of *The Kingdom*, exulting that the spiritual treatise was "now so ably translated into English."[3]

This took place years before Merton's "Seven Storey Mountain" was released to the public, so his name did not yet hold great value to the publishers. In the spirit of humility and silence, Merton accepted for his translation to be attributed simply to "A Trappist Father in The Abbey of Our Lady of Gethsemani."[4]

1   Thomas Merton, *The Seven Storey Mountain* (New York: Harcourt, Brace & Company, 1948), 401.
2   Benjamin Clark, OCSO, "Thomas Merton's Gethsemani: Part 1, the Novitiate Years," *The Merton Annual, vol. 4* (1991): 250.
3   Fulton J Sheen, Introduction to *The Life and Kingdom of Jesus in Christian Souls,* by St. John Eudes (New York: PJ Kennedy & Sons, 1946), xix.
4   The attribution to a "Trappist *father*" is curious given that Merton would not be ordained until 1949. However, there is no doubt that the work is his. Fr. Benjamin Clark OCSO was the "other novice" referred to in the Seven Storey Mountain. Fr. Clark recalls:
   "I remember one such assignment which Merton records (SSM, p. 401). Gethsemani had entered a contract to translate the work of St. John Eudes for the publication of a new edition. Several of the monks had been assigned volumes to translate, and Merton was given The Kingdom of Jesus in Christian Souls. The publishers had allowed only a short time for the work to be completed and so I was assigned to help Merton meet the deadline. I typed the finished copy in triplicate as Merton dashed off the original on sheets of yellow paper." "Thomas Merton's Gethsemani," p. 249.

About St. John Eudes

Born in France on November 14, 1601, St. John Eudes' life spanned the "Great Century." The Age of Discovery had revolutionized technology and exploration; the Council of Trent initiated a much-needed reform in the Church; among the common people, it was the dawn of a golden age of sanctity and mystic fervor.

His Spiritual Heritage

No fewer than seven Doctors of the Church had lived in the previous century. Great reformers like St. Francis de Sales, St. Teresa of Avila, and St. John of the Cross had left an indelible mark on the Catholic faith. Their influence was still fresh as St. John Eudes came onto the scene.

He was educated by the Jesuits in rural Normandy. He was ordained into the Oratory of Jesus and Mary, a society of priests which had just been founded on the model of St. Philip Neri's Oratory in Rome. The founder was Cardinal Pierre de Bérulle, a man renowned for his holiness and named "the apostle of the Incarnate Word" by Pope Urban VII. Rounding out St. John Eudes' heritage is the influence of the Discalced Carmelites. His spiritual director, Cardinal Bérulle himself, had brought sisters from St. Teresa of Avila's convent to help found the Carmel in France. John Eudes would later become spiritual director to a Carmelite convent himself. Their cloister prayed constantly for his missionary activity.

His Life of Ministry

As an avid participant in a wave of re-evangelization in France, St. John Eudes' principal apostolate was preaching parish missions. Spending anywhere from 4 to 20 weeks in each parish, he preached over 120 missions across his lifetime, always with a team of confessors providing the sacrament around the clock, and catechists meeting daily with small groups of parishioners.

Early in his priesthood, an outbreak of plague hit St. John Eudes' native region and he rushed to provide sacraments to the dying. The risk of contagion was so great no one else dared to approach the victims. In order to protect his Oratorian brothers from contagion, St. John Eudes took up residence in a large empty cider barrel outside of the city walls until the plague had ended.

His Foundations

During his missions he heard countless confessions himself, including those from women forced into prostitution. Realizing that they needed intense healing and support, he began to found "Houses of Refuge" to help them get off the street and begin a new life. In 1641 he founded the Sisters of Our Lady of Charity of the Refuge to continue this work. They would live with the penitent women and provide them with constant support. Today, these sisters are known as the Good Shepherd Sisters, inspired by their fourth vow of zeal to go out seeking the "lost sheep."

Occasionally, St. John Eudes would return to the site of a previous mission. To his dismay, he found that the fruits of the mission were consistently fading for lack of support. The crucial piece in need of change was the priesthood. At that time, the only way to be trained as a priest was through apprenticeship. The result of this training was so horribly inconsistent that the term "hocus pocus" was invented during this time to describe the corrupted Latin used by poorly trained priests during the consecration at mass. In 1643 he left the Oratory and founded the Congregation of Jesus and Mary to found a seminary. Seminary training was a radical brand-new concept which had just been proposed by the Council of Trent.

His Mark on the Church

At a mission in 1648 St. John Eudes authored the first mass in history in honor of the Heart of Mary. In 1652 he built the first church under the Immaculate Heart's patronage: the chapel of his seminary in Coutances, France. During the process of his canonization, Pope St. Pius X named St. John Eudes "the father, doctor, and apostle of liturgical devotion to the hearts of Jesus and Mary." The Heart of Jesus because he created the first Feast of the Sacred Heart in 1672, just one year before St. Margaret Mary Alacoque had her first apparition of the Sacred Heart.

Although his Marian devotion was intense from a tender age, the primary inspiration for this feast came from St. John Eudes' theology of baptism. From the beginning of his missionary career he taught that Jesus continues His Incarnation in the life of each baptized Christian. As we give ourselves to Christ, our hands become His hands, our heart is transformed into His heart. Mary is the ultimate exemplar of this. She gave her heart to God so completely that she and Jesus have just one heart between them. Thus, whoever sees Mary, sees Jesus, and honoring the heart of Mary is never separate from honoring the heart of Jesus.

Doctor of the Church?

At the time of this writing, Bishops the world over have requested that the Vatican proclaim St. John Eudes as a Doctor of the Church. This would recognize his unique contribution to our understanding of the Gospel, and his exemplary holiness of life which stands out even among saints. For more information on the progress of this cause, on his writings or spirituality, or to sign up for our e-newsletter updates, contact spirituality@eudistsusa.org.

About the Eudist Family

During his lifetime, St. John Eudes' missionary activity had three major areas of focus.
- For priests, he provided formation, education, and the spiritual support which is crucial for their role in God's plan of salvation.
- For prostitutes and others on the margins of society, he gave them a home and bound their wounds, like the Good Shepherd with his lost sheep.
- For the laity, he preached the dignity of their baptism and their responsibility to be the hands and feet of God, to continue the Incarnation.

In everything he did, he burned with the desire to be a living example of the love and mercy of God.

These are the "family values" which continue to inspire those who continue his work. To paraphrase St. Paul, John Eudes planted seeds, which others watered through the institutions he founded, and God gave the growth. Today, the family tree continues to bear fruit:

The *Congregation of Jesus and Mary* (CJM), also known as The Eudists, continues the effort to form and care for priests and other leaders within the Church. St. John Eudes called this the mission of "teaching the teachers, shepherding the shepherds, and enlightening those who are the light of the world." Continuing his efforts as a missionary preacher, Eudist priests and brothers "audaciously seek to open up new avenues for evangelization," through television, radio, and new media.

The *Religious of the Good Shepherd* (RGS) continue outreach to women in difficult situations, providing them with a deeply needed place of refuge and healing while they seek a new life. St. Mary Euphrasia drastically expanded the reach of this mission which now operates in over 70 countries worldwide. A true heiress of St. John Eudes, St. Mary Euphrasia exhorted her sisters: "We must go after the lost sheep with no other rest than the cross, no other consolation than work, and no other thirst than for justice."

In every seminary and House of Refuge founded by St. John Eudes, he also established a *Confraternity of the Holy Heart of Jesus and Mary* for the laity, now known as the Eudist Associates. The mission he gave them was twofold: First, "To glorify the divine Hearts of Jesus and Mary... working to make them live and reign in their own heart through diligent imitation of their virtues." Second, "To work for the salvation of souls... by practicing, according to their abilities, works of charity and mercy and by attaining numerous graces through prayer for the clergy and other apostolic laborers."

The *Little Sisters of the Poor* were an outgrowth of this confraternity. St. Jeanne Jugan was formed as a consecrated woman within the Eudist Family. She discovered the great need for love and mercy among the poor and elderly and the mission took on a life of its own. She passed on to them the Eudist intuition that the poor are not simply recipients of charity, they provide an encounter with Charity Himself: "My little ones, never forget that the poor are Our Lord... In serving the aged, it is He Himself whom you are serving."

A more recent "sprout" on the tree was founded by Mother Antonia Brenner in Tijuana, Mexico. After raising her children in Beverly Hills and suffering through divorce, she followed God's call to become a live-in prison minister at the *La Mesa* penitentiary. The *Eudist Servants of the 11th Hour* was founded so that other women in the latter part of their lives could imitate her in "being love" to those most in need.

The example St. John Eudes set for living out the Gospel has inspired many more individuals and organizations throughout the world. For more information about the Eudist family, news on upcoming publications, or for ways to share in our mission, contact us at spirituality@eudistsusa.org.

On the Threshold of Life: A Self-Directed Retreat to Celebrate your Birthday

For more from St. John Eudes, Eudist Press offers individual prayerbooks that shine a spotlight on different aspects of his spirituality. Each one is an excerpt from his classic bestseller: *The Life and the Kingdom of Jesus: A Treatise on Christian Perfection for Use by Clergy or Laity,* translated from French by Thomas Merton in The Abbey of Our Lady of Gethsémani and published by Kennedy & Sons in New York, 1946.

They can be found at https://www.eudistsusa.org/publications.

More by Eudist Press
- *A Heart on Fire: St. John Eudes, a Model for the New Evangelization*
- *Spiritual Itinerary for Today with St. John Eudes*
- *Eudist Lectionary: A St. John Eudes Reader*

Eudist Prayerbook Series
- Volume 1: *Heart of the Holy Family: A Manual of Prayer*
- Volume 2: *More than Just 50 Beads: Rosary Meditations for the Liturgical Year*
- Volume 3: *A Holy Week Every Week: Weekday Meditations*
- Volume 4: *34 Flames of Divine Love: Elevations of the Heart Towards God*
- Volume 5: *On the Threshold of Life: A Self-Directed Retreat to Celebrate your Birthday*
- Volume 6: *On the Threshold of Eternity: A Self-Directed Retreat to Prepare for a Happy Death*

Biography
- *St. John Eudes: An Artisan of Christian Renewal of the Seventeenth Century*
- *In All Things, the Will of God: St. John Eudes Through His Letters*

More by St. John Eudes
St. John Eudes' Selected Works
- *The Life and Kingdom of Jesus in Christian Souls*
- *The Sacred Heart of Jesus*
- *The Admirable Heart of Mary*
- *The Priest: His Dignity and Obligations*
- *Meditations*
- *Letters and Shorter Works*

Other Works
- *Man's Contract with God in Holy Baptism*
- *The Wondrous Childhood of the Mother of God*

www.ingramcontent.com/pod-product-compliance
Lightning Source LLC
Chambersburg PA
CBHW041755040426
42446CB00001B/42